EPIC

THE STORY
GOD IS TELLING
and the ROLE THAT IS
YOURS TO PLAY

JOHN ELDREDGE

NELSON BOOKS
A Division of Thomas Nelson Publishers
Since 1798

www.thomasnelson.com

Published in Nashville, Tennessee, by Thomas Nelson, Inc.

Published in association with Yates & Yates, LLP, Attorneys and Counselors, Orange, California.

Bible translations used are referenced at the back of the book.

Library of Congress Cataloging-in-Publication Data

Eldredge, John.
    Epic : the story God is telling and the role that is yours to play / John Eldredge.
        p. cm.
    ISBN 0-7852-6531-7
    1. Christian life I. Title.
    BV4501.3.E42 2004
    231.7—dc22

                                                    2004014403

Printed in the United States of America

05 06 07 08 WRZ 9 8 7 6 5

CONTENTS

I had always felt life first as a story—
and if there is a story there is a story teller.
—G. K. CHESTERTON

PROLOGUE

"I wonder what sort of tale we've fallen into?"
— J. R. R. TOLKIEN, *The Lord of the Rings*

It's been quite a journey for Frodo and Sam when the little gardener wonders this. Ever since they left home they've encountered more wonders and more dangers than they could have possibly imagined. The battle on Weathertop. The flight to the ford. The beauty of Rivendell. The dark mines of Moria, where they lost their beloved Gandalf. Their fellowship has fallen apart; their friends are now far away on another part of the journey. Into the shadow of Mordor they've come, two little hobbits and their cooking gear on a journey to save the world.

It's at this point Sam says, "I wonder what sort of

tale we've fallen into?" Sam could not have asked a better question.

He assumes that there *is* a story; there is something larger going on. He also assumes that they have somehow tumbled into it, been swept up into it.

What sort of tale have I fallen into? is a question that would help us all a great deal if we wondered it for ourselves.

It just might be the most important question we ever ask.

LIFE IS A STORY

Life, you'll notice, is a story.

Life doesn't come to us like a math problem. It comes to us the way that a story does, scene by scene. You wake up. What will happen next? You don't get to know—you have to enter in, take the journey as it comes. The sun might be shining. There might be a tornado outside. Your friends might call and invite you to go sailing. You might lose your job.

Life unfolds like a drama. Doesn't it? Each day has a beginning and an end. There are all sorts of characters, all sorts of settings. A year goes by like a chapter from a novel. Sometimes it seems like a tragedy. Sometimes like a comedy. Most of it feels like a soap opera. Whatever happens, it's a story through and through.

"All of life is a story," Madeleine L'Engle reminds us.

This is helpful to know. When it comes to figuring out this life you're living, you'd do well to know the rest of the story.

You come home one night to find that your car has been totaled. Now, all you know is that you loaned it for a couple of hours to a friend or your teenage daughter, and now here it is, all smashed up. Isn't the first thing out of your mouth, "What *happened?*"

In other words, "Tell me the story."

Somebody has some explaining to do, and that can be done only in hearing the tale *they* have to tell. Careful now—you might jump to the wrong conclusion. Doesn't it make a difference to know that she wasn't speeding, that in fact the other car ran a red light? It changes the way you feel about the whole thing. Thank God, she's all right.

Truth be told, you need to know the rest of the story if you want to understand just about anything in life. Jokes are like that. There's nothing to them at all if you walk in on the punch line. "Then she said, 'That's not my dog!'" Everyone else is in stitches. What is so dang funny? I think I missed something.

Love affairs, layoffs, the collapse of empires, your

child's day at school—none of it makes sense without a story.

STORY IS HOW WE FIGURE THINGS OUT

Bring two people together, and they will soon be telling stories. A child on her grandmother's lap. Two men in a fishing boat. Strangers stuck another hour in an airport. Simply run into a friend. What do you want to know? "How was your weekend?" "Fine" is not a good answer. It's just not satisfying. You heard something about a mariachi band, a fifth of tequila, and a cat. And you want to know more about *that* story.

Look at our fixation with the news. Every morning and every evening, in every part of the globe, billions of people read a paper or tune in to the news. Why? Because we humans have this craving for meaning—for the rest of the story. We need to know what's going on.

Our boys are ambushed somewhere in Asia. What's happening over there? A virus is rampaging on the Internet. What do we need to do to protect ourselves? Somehow we don't feel as lost if we know what's going on around us. We want to feel oriented to our world. When we turn on the news, we are tuning in to a world of stories. Not just facts—stories.

Story is the language of the heart.

After all, what's the world's favorite way to spend a Friday night? With a story—a book, a favorite show, a movie. Isn't it true? Good grief! There's a video store on every corner now. They've taken the place of neighborhood churches.

It goes far deeper than entertainment, by the way. Stories nourish us. They provide a kind of food that the soul craves. "Stories are equipment for living," says Hollywood screenwriting teacher Robert McKee. He believes that we go to the movies because we hope to find in someone else's story something that will help us understand our own. We go "to live in a fictional reality that illuminates our daily reality."

Stories shed light on our lives.

We might know that life is a journey, but through Frodo's eyes, we see what that journey will require. We might know that courage is a virtue, but having watched Maximus in *Gladiator* or Jo March in *Little Women*, we find ourselves longing to be courageous. We learn all of our most important lessons through story, and story deepens all of our most important lessons.

As Daniel Taylor has written, "Our stories tell us who we are, why we are here, and what we are to do.

They give us our best answers to all of life's big questions, and to most of the small ones as well."

This is why, if you want to get to know someone, you need to know *their* story. Their life is a story. It, too, has a past and a future. It, too, unfolds in a series of scenes over the course of time. Why is Grandfather so silent? Why does he drink too much? Well, let me tell you. There was a terrible battle in World War II, in the South Pacific, on an island called Okinawa. Tens of thousands of American men died or were wounded there; some of them were your grandfather's best friends. He was there, too, and saw things he has never been able to forget.

"But in order to make you understand," explained novelist Virginia Woolf, "to give you my life, I must tell you a story."

I expect all of us, at one time or another, in an attempt to understand our lives or discover what we ought to do, have gone to someone else with our stories. This is not merely the province of psychotherapists and priests, but of any good friend. "Tell me what happened. Tell me your story, and I'll try to help you make some sense of it."

You seem . . . stuck. Things fall apart. What does it all mean? Should you have chosen a different major after all? Were you meant to take that teaching job? Are you going to find someone to spend your life with, and will he or she remain true? What about the kids—are they headed in the right direction? Did you miss an opportunity in their lives, some key moment along the way? And if crucial moments are about to happen, will you recognize them? Will you miss your cues?

We humans share these lingering questions: "Who am I really? Why am I here? Where will I find life? What does God want of me?" The answers to these questions seem to come only when we know the rest of the story.

As Neo said in *The Matrix Reloaded*, "I just wish I knew what I am supposed to do." If life is a story, what is the plot? What is your role to play? It would be good to know that, wouldn't it? What is this all about?

"Seeing our lives as stories is more than a powerful metaphor," wrote Taylor. "It is how experience presents itself to us."

WE HAVE LOST OUR STORY

And here's where we run into a problem.

For most of us, life feels like a movie we've arrived at forty-five minutes late.

Something important seems to be going on . . .
maybe. I mean, good things do happen, sometimes
beautiful things. You meet someone, fall in love. You
find that work that is yours alone to fulfill. But tragic
things happen too. You fall out of love, or perhaps the
other person falls out of love with you. Work begins
to feel like a punishment. Everything starts to feel
like an endless routine.

If there is meaning to this life, then why do our
days seem so *random?* What is this drama we've been
dropped into the middle of? If there is a God, what
sort of story is he telling here? At some point we
begin to wonder if Macbeth wasn't right after all: Is
life a tale "told by an idiot, full of sound and fury, signifying nothing"?

No wonder we keep losing heart.

We find ourselves in the middle of a story that is
sometimes wonderful, sometimes awful, often a confusing mixture of both, and we haven't a clue how to
make sense of it all. It's like we're holding in our
hands some pages torn out of a book. These pages are
the days of our lives. Fragments of a story. They seem
important, or at least we long to know they are, but
what does it all mean? If only we could find the book
that contains the rest of the story.

Chesterton had it right when he said, "With every

step of our lives we enter into the middle of some story which we are certain to misunderstand."

The world has lost its story. How that happened is quite a story as well, one we haven't time for here. But the latest chapter of that story had to do with the modern era and how mankind looked to science to solve the riddle of our lives. As Neil Postman said about the scientific view:

> In the end, science does not provide the answers most of us require. Its story of our origins and our end is, to say the least, unsatisfactory. To the question, "How did it all begin?", science answers, "Probably by an accident." To the question, "How will it all end?", science answers, "Probably by an accident." And to many people, the accidental life is not worth living. *(Science and the Story That We Need)*

Since then we've pretty much given up on trying to find any larger story in which to live. We've settled for *un*certainty—we can't really know. Listen to the way people offer their thoughts or opinions on just about anything these days. They always start or finish a sentence with a qualifying comment like this: "But that's just the way I see it."

That's not merely a show of humility. It's a sign of our shared belief that nothing certain can be known. All we have now are our opinions. "The lost sense," poet David Whyte observed, "that we play out our lives as part of a greater story."

> It was one of those great stories
> That you can't put down at night
> The hero knew what he had to do
> And he wasn't afraid to fight
> The villain goes to jail
> And the hero goes free
> I wish it were that simple for me.
> (Phil Collins and David Crosby, "Hero")

What sort of tale *have* we fallen into?

THERE IS A LARGER STORY

Walk into any large mall, museum, amusement park, university, or hospital, and you will typically meet at once a very large map with the famous red star and the encouraging words *You are here*. These maps are offered to visitors as ways to orient themselves to their situation, get some perspective on things. This is the Big Picture. This is where you are in that picture.

Hopefully you now know where to go. You have your bearings.

Oh, that we had something like this for our lives.

"This is the Story in which you have found yourself. Here is how it got started. Here is where it went wrong. Here is what will happen next. Now this—this is the role you've been given. If you want to fulfill your destiny, this is what you must do. These are your cues. And here is how things are going to turn out in the end."

We can.

We can discover *the* Story. Maybe not with perfect clarity, maybe not in the detail that you would like, but in greater clarity than most of us now have, and that would be worth the price of admission. I mean, to have some clarity would be gold right now. Wouldn't it?

Start with the movies you love.

I'm serious. Think about your favorite movies. Notice that every good story has the same ingredients. Love. Adventure. Danger. Heroism. Romance. Sacrifice. The Battle of Good and Evil. Unlikely heroes. Insurmountable odds. And a little fellowship that in hope beyond hope pulls through in the end.

Am I right? Think again about your favorite movies. *Sense and Sensibility. Don Juan DeMarco. Titanic. The Sound of Music. Sleepless in Seattle. Gone with the Wind. Braveheart. Gladiator. Rocky. Top Gun. Apollo 13. The*

Matrix. The Lord of the Rings. The films you love are telling you something very important, something essential about your *heart.*

Most of us haven't stopped to ask ourselves, *Now why* that *heart? Why* those *longings and desires?* Might we have been given our longings for love and adventure, for romance and sacrifice as a kind of clue, a treasure map to the meaning of Life itself?

Next, I want you to notice that all the great stories pretty much follow the same story line. Things were once good, then something awful happened, and now a great battle must be fought or a journey taken. At just the right moment (which feels like the last possible moment), a hero comes and sets things right, and life is found again.

It's true of every fairy tale, every myth, every Western, every epic—just about every story you can think of, one way or another. *Braveheart, Titanic,* the *Star Wars* series, *Gladiator, The Lord of the Rings* trilogy. They pretty much all follow the same story line.

Have you ever wondered why?

Every story, great and small, shares the same essential structure because every story we tell borrows its power from a Larger Story, a Story woven into the fabric of our being—what pioneer psychologist Carl Jung tried to explain as archetype, or what his more recent popularizer Joseph Campbell called myth.

All of these stories borrow from *the* Story. From Reality. We hear echoes of it through our lives. Some secret written on our hearts. A great battle to fight, and someone to fight for us. An adventure, something that requires everything we have, something to be shared with those we love and need.

There is a Story that we just can't seem to escape. There *is* a Story written on the human heart.

As Ecclesiastes has it,

> He has planted eternity in the human heart.
> (3:11 NLT)

Look, wouldn't it make sense that if we ever *did* find the secret to our lives, the secret to the universe, it would come to us first as a story? Story is the very nature of reality. Like the missing parts of a novel, it would explain these pages we are holding, the chapters of our lives.

Second, it would speak to our hearts' deepest desires. If nature makes nothing in vain, then why the human heart? Why those universal longings and desires? The secret simply couldn't be true unless it contained the best parts of the stories that you love.

Yet it would also need to go deeper and higher than any of them alone.

EPIC

Christianity claims to do that for us.

Not the Christianity of proper church attendance and good manners. Not the Christianity of holier-than-thou self-righteousness and dogmatism. Not another religion, thank God.

That is not Christianity. Oh, I know it's what most people, including the majority of Christians, think Christianity is all about. They are wrong. There is more. *A lot more.* And that more is what most of us have been longing for most of our lives.

A Story. An Epic.

Something hidden in the ancient past.

Something dangerous now unfolding.

Something waiting in the future for us to discover.

Some crucial role for us to play.

Christianity, in its true form, tells us that there is an Author and that he is good, the essence of all that is good and beautiful and true, for he is the source of all these things. It tells us that he has set our hearts' longings within us, for he has made us to live in an Epic. It warns that the truth is always in danger of being twisted and corrupted and stolen from us because there is a Villain in the Story who hates our hearts and wants to destroy us. It calls us up into a Story that is truer and deeper than any other, and assures us that there we will find the meaning of our lives.

What if?

What if all the great stories that have ever moved you, brought you joy or tears—what if they are telling you something about the *true* Story into which you were born, the Epic into which you have been cast?

We won't begin to understand our lives, or what this so-called gospel is that Christianity speaks of, until we understand the Story in which we have found ourselves. For when you were born, you were born into an Epic that has already been under way for quite some time. It is a Story of beauty and intimacy and adventure, a Story of danger and loss and heroism and betrayal.

> It is a world of magic and mystery, of deep darkness and flickering starlight. It is a world where terrible things happen and wonderful things too. It is a world where goodness is pitted against evil, love against hate, order against chaos, in a great struggle where often it is hard

to be sure who belongs to which side because appearances are endlessly deceptive. Yet for all its confusion and wildness, it is a world where the battle goes ultimately to the good, who live happily ever after, and where in the long run everybody, good and evil alike, becomes known by his true name . . . That is the fairy tale of the Gospel with, of course, one crucial difference from all other fairy tales, which is that the claim made for it is that it is true, that it not only happened once upon a time but has kept on happening ever since and is happening still. (Frederick Buechner, *Telling the Truth*)

But I rush ahead. Let's discover the Epic for ourselves.

Act One

ETERNAL LOVE

In the beginning was the Word, and the Word was with God, and the Word was God. He was with God in the beginning.

—JOHN 1:1 2

n the beginning . . ." or "Once upon a time . . ."

It's a wonderful phrase, isn't it, full of legend and myth, promise and mystery, and a sort of *invitation.* "Come, let me show you something . . ."

Once upon a time there were a good king and queen who were very sad because they had no children. Once upon a time there was a beautiful maiden who lived with her wicked stepsisters. Once upon a time, of all the good days of the year, on Christmas Eve. A long time ago, in a galaxy far, far away. All of the really good stories start that way.

It rouses our longing for the ancient things, our insatiable curiosity to look back into ages past. For God has, may I remind you, set eternity in our hearts (Ecclesiastes 3:11). So many stories—and especially the great epics—hearken back to legend and myth and things forgotten. Because *our* Story begins there. Once upon a time.

"In the beginning" is used twice in the Scriptures. There is the well-known passage from Genesis: "In the beginning God created the heavens and the earth" (1:1).

And an important passage it is, to be sure. But to grasp this Epic, you cannot start there. That is way into the Story. That is Act Three. It is a beginning, but it is the beginning of the *human* story, the story of life here on earth. As Hebrew scholar Robert Alter says, a better rendering of the Hebrew goes, "When God began to create heaven and earth." When God began to create the life we know. And before this? There are events that have preceded this chapter, events that we must know.

If you want to look back into the once upon a time *before* all time, well, then you have to start with another passage, from the gospel of John:

> In the beginning was the Word, and the Word
> was with God, and the Word was God. He was
> with God in the beginning. Through him all

things were made; without him nothing was
made that has been made. (1:1–3)

Now we are reaching back to things prior to Genesis.
Once upon eternity, if you will. What does it mean?
John was peering back into the mystery of God's own
life, before anything else existed, and he was trying to
unveil this: in the ancient past there was a fellowship, a
heroic intimacy, something called the Trinity.

Picture the opening scenes of the movie *The Last of
the Mohicans*:

1757.
THE AMERICAN COLONIES.
IT IS THE 3RD YEAR OF THE WAR
BETWEEN ENGLAND AND FRANCE FOR
THE POSSESSION OF THE CONTINENT.

THREE MEN,
THE LAST OF A VANISHING PEOPLE,
ARE ON THE FRONTIER
WEST OF THE HUDSON RIVER.

We behold a vast, untamed wilderness. Mountain
and forest, as far as the eye can see. Beauty. Mystery.
A primeval world. Down into those woods we are

taken, and we discover three men running at full speed through deep forest. Leaping across ravines, racing through the heavy undergrowth, they are clearly on some great mission.

No words are spoken in this scene; no words need to be spoken. It is an image of intimacy and fellowship and adventure. A picture of the Trinity.

Now, I have a confession to make. Ever since I began to believe in God (which has taken place only in my adult life), I have pictured God as . . . alone. Sovereign, powerful, all that. But by himself.

Perhaps the notion sprang from the fact that I felt myself to be alone in the universe. Or perhaps it came from religious images of God seated on a great throne way up there . . . somewhere. How wonderful to discover that God has never been alone. He has always been Trinity—Father, Son, and Holy Spirit. God has always been a fellowship. This whole Story began with something *relational*.

It is no small revelation.

The famous atheist Bertrand Russell suggested that if we could strip away the mystery of this universe and get to the heart of things, what we would probably find there would be a mathematical equation. Something as scientific and impersonal as the origin of everything else. A cold view of our world, to be sure.

But it fails to explain one thing: How can human personality have come from something *im*personal? How can a creature as quirky as your uncle Ed have come from a mathematical equation? It doesn't add up.

The great philosophical question is simply, "How did all this get here?" And not only do we have the unavoidable fact that something *is* here; we have something that is dazzling in its detail and complexity, and beautiful beyond description. Hummingbirds. Kangaroos. The Eagle Nebulae. Tulips. Mangoes. The Serengeti. Morning, noon, and night.

It is impossible that it simply started of its own accord, by an accident. Just as implausible (as the argument goes) that a Swiss watch will come together if you toss a thousand parts in your clothes dryer and start it all banging round.

No, the earth has all the marks of an artist's hand.

This will prove a relief to scientists who have been troubled by the fact that the immutable laws of nature don't seem to be entirely immutable after all. That's what threw poor Einstein for a loop, that relativity thing, and got the rest of us believing that *everything* is relative. Nature was generated not by a computer but by a Person. It is personal in nature. If it seems quirky, it's quirky in the way Mozart's *The Magic Flute* and Van Gogh's *Irises* are quirky. It reflects personality.

Now, add to this the fact that walking about in this world there are characters with unique personalities who universally have a sense of humor and a love of story, and all of them are haunted at some level by a longing to make sense of things. If our origins are impersonal and accidental, then why are we for the most part totally dissatisfied with that answer?

No, only personality begets personality.

But I'm afraid many religious views aren't much better than Russell's. God exists, but only as the Great Mind behind the universe. Aristotle's unmoved mover. The Grand Chess Player moving the pieces on this board. An equally cold and indifferent view of the world, only worse because there is Someone at the helm who is unmoved by human suffering.

As Herman Melville confessed, "The reason the mass of men fear God, and at bottom dislike him, is because they rather distrust his heart, and fancy him all brain, like a watch."

What a difference it makes to find that the heart of all things is, in fact, just that—a Heart. A personality. Or better, a fellowship of hearts. Community. Trinity. In other words, reality is relational to its core.

You simply have to look at people to find this to be true. Whatever else it means to be human, we know beyond doubt that it means to be *relational*.

Aren't the greatest joys and memories of your life associated with family, friendship, or falling in love? Aren't your deepest wounds somehow connected to some*one* also, to a failure of relationship? That you were loved but are no longer, or that you never have been chosen?

One of the deepest of all human longings is the longing to belong, to be a part of things, to be invited in. We want to be part of the fellowship. Where did *that* come from?

So, too, our greatest sorrows stem from losing the ones we love. Byron lamented,

> What is the worst of woes that wait on age?
> What stamps the wrinkle deeper on the brow?
> To view each loved one blotted from life's page,
> And be alone on earth, as I am now.

Loneliness might be the hardest cross we bear. Why else would we have come up with solitary confinement as a form of punishment? We are relational to the core. We are made, as it says in Genesis, in the image of God or, better, in the image of the Trinity: "Let *us* make man in *our* image" (1:26, emphasis added).

Meister Eckhart had it right when he said that we are born out of the laughter of the Trinity.

From the Heart of the universe come our beating hearts. From this Fellowship spring all of our longings for a friend, a family, a fellowship—for someplace to *belong*.

INVITED UP AND IN

I grew up in the suburbs of Los Angeles and found more than my share of trouble as a boy. Perhaps more from desperation than wisdom, my parents found it best to ship me off to the great open spaces of eastern Oregon each summer, to my grandfather's cattle ranch.

It was a schoolboy's dream.

Horses and pickup trucks, rifles and old barns, and a vast country to explore. I'd wake each morning to a new adventure. A fence has broken down and the herd is wandering all over the county? Terrific! Let's saddle up. The old tractor needs to be brought in from the field? I'll do it! Let me do it! Afternoons when my grandfather napped, I would catch frogs or climb the rafters in the barns or wander through the fields.

My grandfather was my hero. I remember riding in his old blue Chevy Apache pickup, Pop in his cowboy hat and leather work gloves, waving at nearly everyone on the road, and they would wave back with a sense of respect. It gave me a settled feeling that someone was in charge, someone strong and loving. Together we rode the pastures and the desert sagebrush, mending fences, tending sick cattle, fishing Huck Finn–style with willow branches and a piece of string. It was a time out of time, summer days without end.

Sunday, however, was my favorite day of the week.

Come Sunday afternoons the chores would be called off, and we'd do what my grandfather called "visiting"—calling on relatives in nearby towns and farms. Though we'd just drop in unannounced, they'd always be glad to see us, and somehow the timing was right so that the rhubarb pie was out of the oven and cooling on the windowsill. Whatever folks were doing, they'd drop everything to sit and chat, telling stories, laughing about this and that, asking me what mischief I'd been into.

Now, here was the best part of it all: I didn't have to invent that story.

It didn't depend on me. It had already been going on, years upon years before I ever existed, a great adventure and a fellowship. A story in which I could be a part. And they *wanted* me to be a part of it. They looked forward to my coming. There were a horse and bridle with my name on them.

That is the promise of Act One.

Something preceded us. Something good. We'd

much rather be included in something grand than
have to create the meaning of our lives. To know that
life, ultimately, doesn't rest on our shoulders, but
invites us up into it.

It came as a great surprise to me as a counselor when
I first discovered that children would much rather know
that their parents loved each other than that they loved
them. But, of course, we need to know that love is real,
that it *endures*, that a world of love is planned for us and
waits for us, and that we can count on it. As Jesus said,

> Father, I want those you have given me to be
> with me where I am, and to see my glory, the
> glory you have given me because you loved me
> before the creation of the world. (John 17:24)

We need to know that love lasts. The reason divorce
is so devastating to children (not to mention grown-
ups) is because it ends the story. Just like that. The past
is lost. The future is uncertain. The pictures come down
off the walls. Certain names are never mentioned again.
The love story is over. You can't count on anything.

Now that I am grown, my greatest joys come not
from the adventures I take alone, but from the adventures I invite my wife and sons into. We climb mountains and canoe rivers and eat an entire package of

Oreos in one sitting. We laugh and talk and wrestle and find more joy in anything because it is *shared*.

"In the beginning . . . ," before the dawn of time. Something immortal, eternal. The glory of the elder days. Like the very best of stories, this Epic we've been born into has a golden past, a veiled mystery.

". . . and the Word was with God, and the Word was God. He was with God in the beginning." A Fellowship. The Heart of all things. Not a lonely universe, but one born out of Love. That is why the self-centered life simply does not work. The world is rigged in such a way (where did *that* come from?) that life does not work when it's all about you.

Frodo could not be a hero unless he was born into a story with many chapters already played out before his own. His moment derives its weight and urgency from the moments that have come before.

"Life itself was in him" (John 1:4 NLT). The Fountain of Life, the Wellspring of the life we seek. Unending, unmeasured, life ever young. There was a Life that existed before our own, an Epic already under way.

Once upon a time.

Act Two

THE ENTRANCE OF EVIL

And there was war in heaven.

—REVELATION 12:7

As we turn the page into Act Two, let me ask you a question:

Why does every story have a villain?

It's hard to think of a tale without one. As children, we learned to fear the Big Bad Wolf and the Troll under the bridge. As we grew older, we discovered more serious villains in the *Star Wars* series—Darth Vader and Darth Maul and Darth Sidious. The Wicked Witch of the West hunted Dorothy. Wallace fought against Longshanks, and Maximus went hand to hand against Commodus. The trinity in *The Last of the Mohicans* had to eventually face

Magua, the black-hearted Huron who betrayed them all.

In *The Fellowship of the Ring*, we come to dread the Dark Lord Sauron, the Orcs that do his bidding, and the Black Riders who hunt poor Frodo and the ring that will give the evil one power to enslave the world.

Every story has a villain because *yours* does.

Though most of you do not live like it.

Most people do not live as though the Story has a Villain, and that makes life very confusing. How have we missed this? All the stories we've been telling about the presence of an evil power in the world, all the dark characters that have sent chills down our spines and given us restless nights—they are spoken to us as *warnings*.

There is evil cast around us.

War. Famine. Betrayal. Murder. Surely we know there is an evil force in this world. Where did it come from? What is its motive? How are we to find refuge from its claws?

Things have happened prior to this life we are living, things you must understand. As Gandalf whispered to Frodo, the two of them huddling by the fire, "That is a chapter of ancient history that which it might be good to recall; for there was sorrow then too, and gathering dark, but great valor, and great deeds that were not wholly vain. One day, perhaps, I will tell you all the tale, or you shall hear it told in full by one who knows it best."

Something happened before our moment on this stage. Before mankind came the angels.

ANGELIC POWER

> On the twenty-fourth day of the first month, as I was standing on the bank of the great river, the Tigris, I looked up and there before me was a man dressed in linen, with a belt of the finest gold around his waist. His body was like chrysolite, his face like lightning, his eyes like flaming torches, his arms and legs like the gleam of burnished bronze, and his voice like the sound of a multitude. (Daniel 10:4–6)

We are not alone.

This universe is inhabited by other beings; we share the stage with other players. Now, angels are back in vogue these days. It has become rather chic to believe in angels, even in circles where it remains an embarrassment to believe in God. We are comforted by the thought that we might be assisted by an angel. Yet com-

fort is not the first emotion recorded of the mortals who
have actually *encountered* a real angel.

> I, Daniel, was the only one who saw the vision;
> the men with me did not see it, but such terror
> overwhelmed them that they fled and hid
> themselves . . . I had no strength left, my face
> turned deathly pale and I was helpless. (vv. 7–8)

Why is it, in nearly every record of angelic visita-
tions, their first words to us mortals are "Fear not . . .
Be not afraid"? These are not Raphael's angels, the
ones you see on valentines—cherubic little children
with golden wings, looking no more dangerous than
the rosy-cheeked members of the local preschool.
Real angels are mighty, glorious, dreadful beings,
more powerful than you can imagine.

> The LORD sent an angel, who annihilated all the
> fighting men and the leaders and officers in the
> camp of the Assyrian king. (2 Chronicles 32:21)

> The LORD sent a plague on Israel . . . and sev-
> enty thousand of the people from Dan to
> Beersheba died. When the angel stretched out
> his hand to destroy Jerusalem, the LORD was

> grieved because of the calamity and said to the
> angel who was afflicting the people, "Enough!
> Withdraw your hand." (2 Samuel 24:15–16)

> "Release the four angels who are bound at the
> great river Euphrates." And the four angels
> who had been kept ready for this very hour and
> day and month and year were released to kill a
> third of mankind. (Revelation 9:14–15)

Hold on, now. What sort of Epic is God telling here?

Why does he set the stage with winged creatures so beautiful and noble that we cannot look upon their faces without falling to our knees, so deadly that armies, cities, entire civilizations fall at the hands of a mere few? Yet there are "ten thousand times ten thousand" cast into this great Story (Daniel 7:10). What might it mean?

Foreshadow

You can learn something about a story by the characters the author writes into it. Knights and a dragon are going to give you a certain kind of tale—a tale that chipmunks and acorns cannot provide. The presence of the Jedi warriors ennobles and endangers those dramas, just as we know something serious is about to unfold when we send the marines or the Special Forces to the coast of some distant land.

What does it mean when God sets the stage with the universe's equivalent of the Navy Seals or the Delta Force? They are powerful, they are armed, and they are dangerous.

Perhaps this Story is not nearly as "safe" as we'd like to believe.

This is precisely what the Bible (and all the stories that echo it) has warned us about all these years: we live in two worlds—or in one world with two halves, part that we can see and part that we cannot. We are urged, for our own welfare, to act as though the unseen world (the rest of reality) is, in fact, more weighty and more real and more dangerous than the part of reality we can see. Here is why.

BETRAYAL AND MUTINY

You were the model of perfection,
full of wisdom and perfect in beauty.
You were in Eden,
the garden of God;
every precious stone adorned you:
ruby, topaz and emerald,
chrysolite, onyx and jasper,

sapphire, turquoise and beryl.
Your settings and mountings were made of gold;
on the day you were created they were prepared.
You were anointed as a guardian cherub,
for so I ordained you.
You were on the holy mount of God;
you walked among the fiery stones.
You were blameless in your ways
from the day you were created
till wickedness was found in you. (Ezekiel 28:12–15)

Standing at the head of the vast legions of angelic hosts (millions, as the biblical record counts) was a captain. The most beautiful, the most powerful of them all. The commander of the armies of God. The guardian of the glory of the Lord. His name was Lucifer. "Son of the morning." Glorious as the sun. Unequaled among his noble peers.

And here is where the Story takes its first dramatic turn.

"Of all bad men religious bad men are the worst. Of all created beings the wickedest is one who originally stood in the immediate presence of God" (C. S. Lewis).

There is a danger for the glorious that the humble never know; a trial for the powerful that the weak never face. You see this in the worst of the dictators, the Hitlers and Stalins, the Maos and Amins—they set themselves up to be idols. They want more than power; they want to be worshiped.

Pride entered Lucifer's heart.

The excellent captain came to believe he was being cheated somehow. He didn't merely want to play a noble role in the Story; he wanted the Story to be about *him*. He coveted the throne; he wanted to be the star. He wanted the worship and adoration for himself.

> Your heart became proud
> on account of your beauty,
> and you corrupted your wisdom
> because of your splendor. (Ezekiel 28:17)

How many stories turn upon a betrayal? How many kingdoms have fallen to a coup or a bloody revolt?

Though Maximus was named heir to the throne, jealous Commodus committed murder and seized power for himself. Posing as a Mohican, a friend and guide, Magua betrayed the king's armies and led them into an ambush. The greatest of all the Jedi, Anakin Skywalker turned to the dark side and became Darth Vader. Saruman the White, onetime ally of the free peoples of Middle Earth, lusted for power and vainglory, and thus his ruin, and the ruin of many.

There in the palaces of heaven, in the very court-
yards of happiness and glory unstained, Lucifer
turned on his Maker. Through treachery and deceit,
he drew to his side one-third of the angels, and they
rose up in arms against their sovereign Lord. And
there was war in heaven.

> How shall I relate
> To human sense th' invisible exploits
> Of warring spirits? how, without remorse,
> The ruin of so many, glorious once
> And perfect while they stood.

In *Paradise Lost*, John Milton wrestled with human
language to capture the drama of the scene. As you
read this you might remember any of the great battles
from *The Lord of the Rings*.

> Arms on armor clashing brayed
> Horrible discord . . . dire was the noise
> Of conflict; overhead the dismal hiss
> Of fiery darts in flaming volleys flew . . .
> So under fiery cope together rushed
> Both battles main with ruinous assault
> And inextinguishable rage. All heaven
> Resounded; and, had earth been then, all earth

Had to her centre shook.
 . . . Deeds of eternal fame
Were done, but infinite; for wide was spread
That war, and various; sometimes on firm ground
A standing fight; then, soaring on main wing
Tormented all the air; and all air seemed then
Conflicting fire. Long time in even scale
The battle hung, till Satan, . . .
No equal, ranging through the dire attack
Of fighting seraphim confused, at length
Saw where the sword of Michael smote, and felled
Squadrons at once; with huge two-handed sway
Brandished aloft, the horrid edge came down
Wide wasting.

Satan makes his way through the fury of the warring
armies to face the great archangel Michael, who takes
his place at the head of the faithful. There on the field
of battle the mighty captains meet. Michael turns and
confronts the Traitor, Lucifer:

Author of evil, unknown till thy revolt, . . .
 . . . how hast thou disturbed
Heaven's blessed peace, and unto Nature brought
Misery, uncreated till the crime
Of thy rebellion? How hast thou instilled

Thy malice into thousands, once upright
And faithful, now proved false . . .
Heaven casts thee out.

But words will not suffice. The warriors begin to
slowly circle each other, rising up, up into the air to
strike a final blow.

They ended parle, and both addressed for fight
Unspeakable . . . for like gods they seemed,
Stood they or moved, in stature, motion, arms,
Fit to decide the empire of great Heaven.
Now waved their fiery swords, and in the air
Made horrid circles; two broad suns their shields
Blazed opposite, while Expectation stood
In horror . . . one stroke they aimed
That might determine, and not need repeat . . .
. . . But the sword
Of Michael from the armory of God
Was given him tempered so, that neither keen
Nor solid might resist that edge: it met
The sword of Satan, with steep force to smite
Descending, and in half cut sheer; nor stayed,
But, with swift wheel reverse, deep entering, sheared
All his right side. Then Satan first knew pain.

So Commodus was thrown down in the arena; so Darth Vader was hurled spinning into space; so the trinity foiled Magua's first assault, and he fled into the wilderness. So in ages long, long before Frodo and the Shire, Isildur cut the ring from Sauron's hand and the evil one was vanquished, disappearing for centuries until he could gather his strength once more.

> I drove you in disgrace from the mount of God,
> and I expelled you, O guardian cherub,
> from among the fiery stones. (Ezekiel 28:16)

So evil entered the Story.

I am staggered by the level of naïveté that most people live with regarding evil. They don't take it seriously. They don't live as though the Story has a Villain. Not the devil prancing about in red tights, carrying a pitchfork, but the incarnation of the very worst of every enemy you've met in every other story. Dear God—the Holocaust, child prostitution, terrorist bombings, genocidal governments. What is it going to take for us to take evil seriously?

Life is very confusing if you do not take into account that there is a Villain. That you, my friend, have an Enemy.

> One of the things that surprised me when I first read the New Testament seriously was that it talked so much about a Dark Power in the universe—a mighty evil spirit who was held to be the Power behind death, disease, and sin . . . Christianity thinks this Dark Power was created by God, and was good when he was created, and went wrong. Christianity agrees . . . this is a universe at war. (C. S. Lewis, *Mere Christianity*)

Satan mounted his rebellion through the power of an idea: God is holding out on us. After their insurrection was squelched, and they were hurled from the high walls of heaven, that question lingers like smoke from a forest fire: Is God truly good? Is he holding out on us?

Yes, God and his angels won. Through force of arms. But power is not the same thing as Goodness. Anyone who has met a bully knows this. Just because you're stronger doesn't mean you can be trusted. At the end of Act Two, Evil has entered the story in dreadful form, and God's own heart has been called into question.

Now the stage is set for Act Three.

Act Three

THE BATTLE FOR THE HEART

When God began to create the heaven and earth . . .
— GENESIS 1:1 (*Alter*)

ct Three begins in darkness.

Darkness over the deep and God's breath hovering over the waters. (Genesis 1:2, *Alter*)

Like the hush in the darkness before the first notes of a concert or symphony. Or perhaps like the darkness of your bedroom in the very early hours, just before you open your eyes, right before someone flings opens the curtains to the new day. And not just any day. The first day of vacation.

"Hush!" said the Cabby. They all listened.

In the darkness something was happening at last. A voice had begun to sing. It was very far away and Digory found it hard to decide from what direction it was coming. Sometimes it seemed to come from all directions at once. Sometimes he almost thought it was coming out of the earth beneath them . . . But it was, beyond comparison, the most beautiful noise he had ever heard. It was so beautiful he could hardly bear it . . .

Then two wonders happened at the same moment. One was that the voice was suddenly joined by other voices; more voices than you could possibly count. They were higher up in the scale: cold, tingling, silvery voices. The second wonder was that the blackness overhead, all at once, was blazing with stars. They didn't come out gently, one by one, as they do on a summer evening. One moment there had been nothing but darkness; next moment a thousand, thousand points of light leaped out—single stars, constellations, and planets, brighter and bigger than any in our world. There were no clouds. The new stars and the new voices began at exactly the same time. If you had heard it, as

> Digory did, you would have felt quite certain
> that it was the stars themselves which were
> singing, and that it was the First Voice, the deep
> one, which had made them appear and made
> them sing.
>
> "Glory be!" said the Cabby. "I'd ha' been a better
> man all my life if I'd known there were things
> like this." (C. S. Lewis, *The Magician's Nephew*)

Suddenly a voice breaks the silence, and there is light.

Another word is spoken, and the great canopy of
the heavens is unfurled, a sky more blue than you've
ever seen it, yet translucent when it is dark to reveal
the stars that lie beyond.

Yet another word, and the seas draw back to reveal
the land masses of earth.

Again a word, and mangoes laden the branches of
their trees, blackberries burst forth on the bushes,
cabernet grapes drip from the vine, fields of sun-
flowers stand upright, their happy faces to the new
sun. And the sun—a whirling ball of fire balanced in
the heavens just close enough to warm the new earth,
yet not too close to do us harm.

> The lion was pacing to and fro . . . And as he
> walked and sang the valley grew green with

grass. It spread out from the lion like a pool. It ran up the sides of the little hills like a wave. In a few minutes it was creeping up the lower slopes of the distant mountains, making that young world every moment softer. The light wind could now be heard ruffling the grass. Soon there were other things besides grass. The higher slopes grew dark with heather. Patches of rougher and more bristling green appeared in the valley. Digory did not know what they were until one began coming up quite close to him. It was a little, spiky thing that threw out dozens of arms and covered these arms with green and grew larger at the rate of about an inch every two seconds. There were dozens of these things all round him now. When they were as nearly as tall as himself he saw what they were. "Trees!" he exclaimed. *(The Magician's Nephew)*

If you learned about Eden in Sunday school, with poster board and flannel graphs, you missed something. Imagine the most beautiful scenes you have ever known on this earth—rain forests, the prairie in full bloom, storm clouds over the African savanna, the Alps under a winter snow. Then imagine it all on the day it was born.

It's Tolkien's Shire in its innocence, Iguazu Falls in

the garden of *The Mission*, the opening scene of *The Lion King*.

And it doesn't stop there.

Into this world God opens his hand, and the animals spring forth. Myriads of birds, in every shape and size and song, take wing—hawks, herons, warblers. All the creatures of the sea leap into it—whales, dolphins, fish of a thousand colors and designs. Thundering across the plains race immense herds of horses, gazelles, buffalo, running like the wind. It is more astonishing than we could possibly imagine. No wonder "the morning stars sang together and all the angels shouted for joy" (Job 38:7). A great hurrah goes up from the heavens!

We have grown dull toward this world in which we live; we have forgotten that it is not *normal* or *scientific* in any sense of the word. It is fantastic. It is fairy tale through and through. Really now. Elephants? Caterpillars? Snow? At what point did you lose your wonder at it all?

Even so, once in a while something will come along and shock us right out of our dullness and resignation.

We come round a corner, and there before us is a cricket, a peacock, a stag with horns as big as he. Perhaps we come upon a waterfall, the clouds have made a rainbow in a circle round the sun, or a mouse scampers across the counter, pauses for a moment to twitch its whiskers at you, and disappears into the cupboard. And for a moment we realize that we were born into a world astonishing as any fairy tale.

A world made for romance.

ROMANCE

Creation unfolds like a great work of art, a masterpiece in the making. And just as you can learn about an author by the stories he tells, you can learn a great deal about an artist from the works he creates. Surely you see that God is more creative than we can possibly imagine, and romantic to the core. Lovers and honey-mooners choose places like Hawaii, the Bahamas, or Tuscany as a backdrop for their love. But whose idea was Hawaii, the Bahamas, or Tuscany?

Let's bring this a little closer to home. Whose idea was it to create the human form in such a way that a kiss could be so delicious? And he didn't stop there, as only lovers know.

Notice how creation builds and swells toward a climax.

It begins with uncut stone or a mass of clay or a rough sketch, "formless and empty" as Genesis 1:2 has it. Then it starts to take shape—light and dark, heavens and earth, land and sea. Large, sweeping movements on a grand scale. Next come the realms of forest and meadow. Tulips and pine trees and moss-covered stones. Color, detail, finer lines. Then follows the animal kingdom in its vast array. Camels, penguins, your cat. Creation is growing in precision and intricacy of form and movement and color. Personality is woven through it all. And it is building to a crescendo.

Then something truly astonishing takes place.

> And God said, "Let us make a human in our own image, by our likeness, to hold sway over the fish of the sea and the fowl of the heavens and the cattle and the wild beasts and all the crawling things that crawl upon the earth." And God created the human in his image, in the image of God He created him, male and female He created them. (Genesis 1:26–27 *Alter*)

Take the best romantic scenes you've ever seen, lift them out of time and space, and you have something of Eden. Remember in *Braveheart*, the rugged William Wallace and the beautiful Murron, riding in the evening on horseback through the Highlands of Scotland, wading through streams, sitting together to talk as if for the very first time.

Picture the lovers on the bow of the *Titanic*, Jack and Rose slicing through an emerald sea, clothed in the colors of a sunset, and their first kiss. Recall *The Fellowship of the Ring*, in the garden of Rivendell, where the Lady Arwen and the great warrior Aragorn steal away to the bridge by the waterfall, in the moonlight, also to share a kiss.

We are haunted by Eden. It finds its way into nearly every story.

Imagine, if you can, that you have never seen this garden planet, and that you have been dropped, suddenly, into the most verdant forest on the earth. Howler monkeys scream in the trees. A chameleon races across the log in front of you. Toucans call to one another in the canopy above. There goes a jaguar. Suddenly, through the ferns, you see something walking along the grassy bank of a stream. Its eyes are bright with intelligence and curiosity, its body unlike anything you have seen. It is singing.

What would you think if you saw a naked man or woman for the first time? All those mythologies about gods and goddesses are not far from the truth.

> My wife's body is brighter and more fascinating than a flower, shier than any animal, and more breathtaking than a thousand sunsets. To

> me her body is the most awesome thing in cre-
> ation. Trying to look at her, just trying to take
> in her wild, glorious beauty . . . I catch a
> glimpse of what it means that men and women
> have been made in the image of God. (Mike
> Mason, *The Mystery of Marriage*)

Earlier in the Story, back in the beginning of our time on earth, a great glory was bestowed upon us. All of us—men and women—were created in the image of God. Fearfully and wonderfully made, as the saying goes. Living icons of the living God. Those who have ever stood before *him* fall to their knees without even thinking, as you find yourself breathless before the Grand Canyon, a sunrise, the cliffs by the sea. That glory was shared with us; we were, in Chesterton's phrase, "statues of God walking about in a Garden," endowed with strength and beauty all our own. All that you ever wished you could be, you were—and more. We were glorious.

> When I look at the night sky and see the work
>   of your fingers—
> the moon and the stars you have set in place—
> what are mortals that you should think of us,
> mere humans that you should care for us?

For you made us only a little lower than God,
and you crowned us with glory and honor.
(Psalm 8:3–5 NLT)

I daresay we've heard a bit about original sin, but
not nearly enough about original glory, which comes
before sin and is deeper to our nature. We were
crowned with glory and honor. Why does a woman
long to be beautiful? Why does a man hope to be
found brave? Because we remember, if only faintly,
that we were once more than we are now.

God creates us in his image, with powers like unto
his own—the ability to reason, to create, to share intimacy, to know joy. He gives us laughter and wonder
and imagination. And above all else, he endows us
with that one quality for which he is most known.

THE GREATEST DIGNITY OF ALL

He enables us to love.

He gives us the greatest treasure in all creation: a
heart. For he intends that we should be his intimate
allies, to borrow Dan Allender's phrase, who join in
the Sacred Circle of intimacy that is the core of the
universe, to share in this great Romance.

Just as we have lost our wonder at the world around

us, we have forgotten what a treasure the human heart is. All of the happiness we have ever known and all of the happiness we hope to find is unreachable without a heart. You could not live or love or laugh or cry had God not given you a heart.

And with that heart comes something that just staggers me.

God gives us the freedom to reject him.

He gives to each of us a will of our own.

Good grief, *why?* He knows what free-willed creatures can do. He has already suffered one massive betrayal in the rebellion of the angels. He knows how we will use our freedom, what misery and suffering, what hell will be unleashed on earth because of our choices. *Why?* Is he out of his mind?

The answer is as simple and staggering as this: if you want a world where love is real, you must allow each person the freedom to choose.

> Power can do everything but the most important thing: it cannot control love . . . In a concentration camp, the guards possess almost unlimited power. By applying force, they can make you renounce your God, curse your family, work without pay, eat human excrement, kill and then bury your closest friend or even

your own mother. All this is within their power. Only one thing is not: they cannot force you to love them. This fact may help explain why God sometimes seems shy to use his power. He created us to love him, but his most impressive displays of miracle—the kind we may secretly long for—do nothing to foster that love. As Douglas John Hall has put it, "God's problem is not that God is not able to do certain things. God's problem is that God loves. Love complicates the life of God as it complicates every life."

(Philip Yancey, *Disappointment with God*)

Any parent or lover knows this: love is chosen. You cannot, in the end, force anyone to love you.

So if you are writing a story where love is the meaning, where love is the highest and best of all, where love is the *point,* then you have to allow each person a choice. You have to allow freedom. You cannot force love. God gives us the dignity of freedom, to choose for or against him (and friends, to ignore him is to choose against him).

This is the reason for what Lewis called the Problem of Pain. Why would a kind and loving God create a world where evil is possible? Doesn't he care about our happiness? Isn't he good? Indeed, he does and he is. He cares so much for our happiness that he endows us with the capacity to love and to be loved, which is the greatest happiness of all.

He endows us with a dignity that is almost unimaginable.

For this creator God is no puppeteer.

> I will call it the Doctrine of Conditional Joy . . . The note of the fairy utterance is always, "You may live in a palace of gold and sapphire, if you do not say the word 'cow.'" Or, "You may live happily with the King's daughter, if you do not show her an onion." The vision always hangs upon a veto. All the dizzy and colossal things conceded depend upon one small thing withheld. All the wild and whirling things that are let loose depend upon one thing that is forbidden . . . In the fairy tale an incomprehensible happiness rests upon an incomprehensible condition. A box is opened, and all evils fly out. A word is forgotten, and cities perish. A lamp is lit, and love flies away. A flower is plucked, and human lives are forfeited. An apple is eaten, and the hope of God is gone. (G. K. Chesterton, *Orthodoxy*)

"Trust me in this one thing," God says to us. "I have given the entire earth to you, for your joy. Explore it; awaken it; take care of it for me. And I have given you one another, for love and romance and friendship. You shall be my intimate allies. But on this one matter, you must trust me. Trust that my heart for you is good, that I am withholding this for a reason. Do not eat of the fruit of the Tree of the Knowledge of Good and Evil . . . or you will die."

And this is where our Story takes its tragic turn.

PARADISE LOST

Now the serpent was more crafty than any of the wild animals the LORD God had made. He said to the woman, "Did God really say, 'You must not eat from any tree in the garden'?"

The woman said to the serpent, "We may eat fruit from the trees in the garden, but God did say, 'You must not eat fruit from the tree that is in the middle of the garden, and you must not touch it, or you will die.'"

"You will not surely die," the serpent said to the woman. "For God knows that when you eat of it your eyes will be opened, and you will be like God, knowing good and evil."

> When the woman saw that the fruit of the
> tree was good for food and pleasing to the
> eye, and also desirable for gaining wisdom,
> she took some and ate it. She also gave some
> to her husband, who was with her, and he ate
> it. (Genesis 3:1–6)

Evil was lurking in that Garden. The mighty angel
had once been glorious as well, more glorious than
we. He was, if you recall, captain of the Lord's armies,
beautiful and powerful beyond compare. But he
rebelled against his Creator, led a great battle against
the forces of heaven, and was cast down. Banished but
not destroyed, he waited in the shadows for an opportunity to take his revenge.

You must understand: the Evil One hates God,
hates anything that reminds him of the glory of God
. . . wherever it exists. Unable to overthrow the
Mighty One, he turned his sights on those who bore
his image.

Satan came into the Garden and whispered to
Adam and Eve—and in them, to all of us—"You cannot trust the heart of God . . . he's holding out on you
. . . you've got to take matters under your control." He
sowed the seed of mistrust in our hearts; he tempted
us to seize control.

It's the same lie he is using in your life today, by the way: "Trusting God is way too risky. You're far too vulnerable. Rewrite the Story. Give yourself a better part. Arrange for your own happiness. Disregard him."

The Evil One lied to us about where true life was found . . . and we believed him.

God gave us the wondrous world as our playground, and he told us to enjoy it fully and freely. Yet despite his extravagant generosity, we had to reach for the one forbidden thing.

And at that moment something in our hearts *shifted*. We reached, and in our reaching we fell from grace.

So Helen betrayed Menelaus and her native Greece, and ran off to Troy with her lover. So Edmund betrayed his brothers and sisters, and all Narnia, and joined sides with the White Witch. So Cypher betrayed Neo and Morpheus and the last of the free world. So Cora fell into the hands of Magua. So Boromir betrayed the fellowship. So the *Titanic* struck an iceberg.

Our glory faded, as Milton said, "faded so soon."

Something has gone wrong with the human race, and we know it. Better said, something has gone wrong *within* the human race. It doesn't take a theologian or a psychologist to tell you that. Read a newspaper. Spend a weekend with your relatives. Pay attention to the movements of your own heart in a single day. Most of the misery we suffer on this planet is the fruit of the human heart gone bad. This glorious treasure has been stained, marred, infected. Sin enters the story and spreads like a computer virus.

By the sixth chapter of Genesis, our downward spiral had reached the point where God himself couldn't bear it any longer.

> The LORD saw how great man's wickedness on the earth had become, and that every inclination of the thoughts of his heart was only evil all the time. The LORD was grieved that he had made man on the earth, and his heart was filled with pain. (Genesis 6:5–6)

Any honest person knows this. We know we are not what we were meant to be.

If we'll stop shifting the blame for just a moment, stop trying to put the onus on some other person or policy or race, if we'll take a naked and frank assessment of ourselves, well then. Most of us will squirm and dodge and admit that perhaps we fall a bit short. If we're truly honest, we'll confess that we have it in us to be the Beast, the wicked stepsister, Scrooge.

Most of the world religions concur on this point.

It's not just the obvious evils like murder and racism and betrayal. Each of us is fraught with fears and suspicions and petty jealousies. We are, above all else, self-centered—the very opposite of how the Trinity lives. You have loved God with all your heart, soul, mind, and strength? You have loved your neighbor as yourself?

Neither have I.

We all fail on the most essential virtue of all, the virtue of Eden: We fail when it comes to loving.

Douglas Coupland wrote in *Life After God:*

> Now—here is my secret:
> I tell it to you with an openness of heart that I doubt I shall ever achieve again, so I pray you are in a quiet room as you hear these words. My secret is that I need God—that I am sick and can no longer make it alone. I need God to help me give, because I no longer seem capable of giving; to help me be kind, as I no longer seem capable of kindness; to help me love, as I seem beyond being able to love.

Something has gone wrong. We know that much. Whatever else we know, whatever else our convictions may be, we know that something has gone terribly wrong with the world, with us, with life.

Haven't you ever wondered, if only for a moment, why life comes nowhere close to the desires that are written in your heart? Where are the beauty, intimacy, and adventure? Why can't we make these things last? The poet George Herbert declared, "I cried when I was born and every day shows why." Dear God—what has happened to our world?

> Things fall apart; the centre cannot hold;
> Mere anarchy is loosed upon the world,
> The blood-dimmed tide is loosed, and everywhere
> The ceremony of innocence is drowned.
> (W. B. Yeats, "The Second Coming")

CAPTIVITY AND RESCUE

The ship has gone down. Coruscant has fallen to the Empire. Rome burns. Winter has come to Narnia. Something is rotten in the state of Denmark. Longshanks has enslaved Scotland. Commodus has committed murder, and Rome has fallen under the rule of its most wicked emperor ever.

This is where most stories take up their tale: The kingdom has been overthrown. Paradise has been lost.

Evil holds sway, or is gathering on the borders of the land, ready to make its final move. Frodo barely makes it out of the Shire with his life and the ring of power. The Nine Black Riders cross the river on midsummer's eve and are hunting down the little hobbit with deadly intent. The future of Middle Earth stands on the edge of a knife.

In the first of another trilogy, Neo is awakened from the death-sleep of the Matrix to discover that the world he thought was real is actually a massive deception cast upon the human race to keep them prisoners. He comes to see that he has lived a lie his entire life, that in fact he is not free at all but a slave of a great evil power. Or as the Scripture has it, "The whole world is under the control of the evil one" (1 John 5:19).

Darth Vader just about has the universe under his fist when a pair of droids fall into the hands of Luke Skywalker. Luke has no idea what is unfolding, what remarkable deeds have been done on his behalf, or what will be required of him in the battle to come. Sitting in a sandstone hut with old Ben Kenobi—he does not know this is the great Jedi Obi-Wan Kenobi—Luke discovers the secret message from the princess: "This is our most desperate hour. Help me, Obi-Wan Kenobi. You're my only hope." Messages are also being sent out from the grand ship undone by an iceberg. *Titanic* is going down, and not everyone is going to make it.

But wait.

Consider also this: every great story has a rescue.

Jack will come to rescue Rose. William Wallace will rise up to rescue Scotland. Luke Skywalker will rescue the princess and then the free peoples of the universe. Nemo's father rescues him. Nathaniel rescues beautiful Cora—not just once, but twice. Neo breaks the power of the Matrix and sets a captive world free. Aslan comes to rescue Narnia. I could name a thousand more. Why does every great story have a rescue?

Because yours does.

On the day Adam and Eve fell from grace, they ran off and hid in the bushes. And God came looking for them. He called to Adam, "Where are you?" (Genesis 3:9). Thus began the long and painful story of God's pursuit of mankind. Though we betrayed him and fell into the hands of the Evil One, God did not abandon us. Even a quick read of the Old Testament would be enough to convince you that *rescue* is God's plan. First with Noah, then with Abraham, and then with the nation Israel, you see God looking for a people who will turn to him from the heart, be his intimate allies once more.

The dramatic archetype is the Exodus, where God goes to war against the Egyptian taskmasters to set his captive people free.

Four hundred years they have languished in a life of despair. Suddenly—blood. Hail. Locusts. Darkness. Death. Plague after plague descends on Egypt like the blows of some unrelenting ax. Pharaoh releases his grip, but only for a moment. The fleeing slaves are pinned against the Red Sea when Egypt makes a last charge, hurtling down on them in chariots. God drowns those soldiers in the sea, every last one of them. Standing in shock and joy on the opposite shore, the Hebrews proclaim, "The LORD is a warrior" (Exodus 15:3). God is a warrior. He has come to rescue us.

And about one day later, they are complaining.

They don't like the food; they don't like the water. The journey of freedom is too hard. They want to go back to Egypt.

Rescuing the human heart is the hardest mission in the world.

The dilemma of the Story is this: we don't know if we *want* to be rescued. We are so enamored with our small stories and our false gods, we are so bound up in our addictions and our self-centeredness and take-it-for-granted unbelief that we don't even know how to cry out for help. And the Evil One has no intention of letting his captives walk away scot-free. He seduces us, deceives us, assaults us—whatever it takes to keep us in darkness.

When you read the prophets of the Old Testament, as Yancey said, you get a glimpse into what it feels like to be God.

> I long to be gracious to you. You are precious and honored in my sight, because I love you. But you are the offspring of adulterers. You have made your bed on a high and lofty hill, forsaking me, you uncovered your bed, you climbed into it and opened it wide. You have been false to me. (From Isaiah)

> I remember the devotion of your youth, how as a bride you loved me . . . What fault did you find in me that you strayed so far from me? You are a swift she-camel running here and there, sniffing the wind in her craving—in her heat who can restrain her? Should I not punish them for this? Should I not avenge myself? I have loved you with an everlasting love; I have drawn you with loving kindness. What have I done to make you hate me so much? (From Jeremiah)

> I will answer you according to your idols [your
> false lovers] in order to recapture your heart.
> (From Ezekiel)

God is filled with the jealousy of a wounded lover.
He has been betrayed time and again.

Like a woman bound to an affair from which she
cannot get free, like a man so corrupted he no longer
knows his own name, the human race is captive in the
worst way possible—we are captives of the heart.

> Their hearts are always going astray. (Hebrews
> 3:10)

The challenge God faces is rescuing a people who
have no idea how captive they are; no real idea how
desperate they are. We know we long for Eden, but we
hesitate to give ourselves back to God in abandoned
trust. We are captivated by the lies of our Enemy.

But God has something up his sleeve.

HERO AND LOVER

Suppose there was a king who loved a humble
maiden. This king was like no other king. Every
statesman trembled before his power. No one

dared breathe a word against him, for he had the strength to crush all opponents. And yet this mighty king was melted by love for a humble maiden. How could he declare his love for her? In an odd sort of way, his kingliness tied his hands. If he brought her to the palace and crowned her head with jewels and clothed her body in royal robes, she would surely not resist—no one dared resist him. But would she love him?

She would say she loved him, of course, but would she truly? Would she be happy at his side? How could he *know?* If he rode to her forest cottage in his royal carriage, with an armed escort waving bright banners, that too would overwhelm her. He did not want a cringing subject. He wanted a lover. (Søren Kierkegaard, *The King and the Maiden*)

He wanted a lover. So the mighty king disguised himself as a beggar and went alone to the maiden's door in the wood to win her heart.

It is a parable of the coming of Jesus of Nazareth.

God himself—the King of all creation—takes on human flesh and enters our Story as one of us. He sets aside his glory, clothes himself with humility, and sneaks into the enemy camp, under cover of night, to whisper words of love to his own: "I have come for you." This is, after all, a love story. "We are born in love, by love, and for love," as Gerald May has said. From the laughter of the Trinity we came, and to the laughter of the Trinity we must return.

> As the Father has loved me, so have I loved you. Now remain in my love. (John 15:9)

God created us in freedom to be his intimate allies, and he will not give up on us. He seeks his allies still. Not religion. Not good church people. Lovers. Allies. Friends of the deepest sort.

> I will give them a heart to know me, that I am the LORD. They will be my people, and I will be their God, for they will return to me with all their heart. (Jeremiah 24:7)

It is the most beautiful of all love stories. On the other hand, Kierkegaard's tale doesn't capture the cost the King will have to pay to ransom his Beloved.

He will have to die to rescue you.

Have you noticed that in the great stories the hero must often die to win the freedom of his beloved?

William Wallace is slowly and brutally tortured for daring to oppose the wicked king. He is executed (upon a cross), and yet his death breaks the grip that darkness has held over Scotland. Neo is the Chosen One, faster and more daring than any other before him. Even so, he is killed—shot in the chest at point-blank range. His death and resurrection shatter the power of the Matrix, set the captives free.

Aslan dies upon the stone table for the traitor Edmund and for all Narnia. Maximus dies in the arena to win the freedom of his friends and all Rome. They are all pictures of an even greater sacrifice.

> The Son of Man . . . [came] to give his life as
> a ransom for many. (Matthew 20:28)

Remember, God warned us back in the Garden that the price of our mistrust and disobedience would be death. Not just a physical death, but a *spiritual* death—to be separated from God and life and all the beauty, intimacy, and adventure forever. Through an act of our own free will, we became the hostages of the Kingdom of Darkness and death. The only way out is ransom.

The coming of Jesus of Nazareth was far more like the opening scenes of *Saving Private Ryan*. A dangerous mission, a great invasion, a daring raid into enemy territory, to save the free world, but also to save one man.

Jesus told a story like that in order to shed light on his own coming: "If a man owns a hundred sheep, and one of them wanders away, will he not leave the ninety-nine on the hills and go to look for the one?" (Matthew 18:12). In the midst of the great invasion, like the storming of the beaches at Normandy, God yet sets his eye on one lost soul. On you.

Historically speaking, Jesus of Nazareth was betrayed by one of his followers, handed over to the Romans by the Jewish religious leaders, and crucified. But there was a Larger Story unfolding in that death. He gave his life willingly to ransom us from the Evil One, to pay the price for our betrayal, and to prove for all time and beyond any shadow of a doubt that the heart of God is good. And that your heart matters to him, matters more than tongue can tell.

> He has rescued us from the dominion of dark-
> ness and brought us into the kingdom of the
> Son he loves, in whom we have redemption, the
> forgiveness of sins. (Colossians 1:13–14)

At this point the Story comes to another hush.

It is the stunned silence of the crowd in the Colosseum at the end of *Gladiator*. Maximus, their hero, has just dealt a mortal blow to the Prince of

Darkness. Commodus has been cast down. But it is a blow that will cost Maximus his life. The callous and bloodthirsty mob is for the first time ever . . . silent. The people are speechless.

It is the same hush that comes over the crowd that had been, only moments earlier, hollering for Wallace's death in *Braveheart*.

It is the hush that comes over the crowd gathered to see the crucifixion of Jesus. If you have seen *The Passion of the Christ*, you'll have some idea what I mean.

Somehow we know that something of immense importance has just taken place. We are speechless. Then a voice speaks. It is a Roman soldier who says,

"Surely this man was the Son of God!" (Mark 15:39)

He gets it. He suddenly understands the Story.

SAVED IN EVERY WAY

A Hero and Lover lays down his life to rescue his Beloved. This is the secret to the success of *Titanic*— the biggest box-office hit in the history of the world, all around the world.

It is, first of all, a love story. Jack *pursues* Rose. He rescues her from a life that is killing her heart. A prisoner to a man she doesn't love in a social circle bound by hypocrisy and betrayal, Rose describes the *Titanic* as her "slave ship." She is a prisoner; in despair she will try to end her life.

When Jack comes to rescue her, it is the first time anyone has ever wanted her for her heart. He sets her free from the small story she was living in and invites her up into beauty, intimacy, and adventure. He takes her to the bow of the ship at sunset, and he asks her, "Do you trust me?"

In the same way, God has been wooing us all our lives, calling us up out of our small stories. As Simone Weil said, he sends to us beauty and affliction, he haunts us with a memory of Eden, and he speaks through every story we've ever loved, calling to our hearts: "Do you trust me? Will you let me come for you?"

And then, Jack gives his life for Rose.

The last thirty minutes of the movie might be one of the most dramatic rescue scenes of all time. Plunging down a labyrinth of flooded hallways, struggling through the rubble of the ship in its death throes, they fight their way out of a nightmare trapped below deck to the pandemonium above. Everywhere they look, passengers and crew are desperate, panicking, drowning. Jack pulls Rose up to the highest point he can find, the stern of the sinking ship, the last refuge from the freezing waters.

But there is no escape aboard *Titanic*.

Just before it makes its final plunge into the North Atlantic, Jack says to Rose, "Do not let go of my hand. This is going to get worse before it gets better. Do not let go."

How awful, how haunting are the scenes of the sea of humanity left to freeze to death in water so cold, as Jack said, it stabs every part of the body like a knife. Everything is gone—the beauty, the romance, the adventure. Paradise is lost. And we know it. More than ever before, we know it. As Chesterton said, we all somehow know that we are the "survivors of a wreck, the crew of a golden ship that had gone down before the beginning of the world." The ship has gone down. We are lost at sea.

Finally it is clear that both cannot share the little piece of floating wreckage they have found, and Jack insists that Rose climb upon it while he slowly succumbs to hypothermia and death.

He dies that she may live.

When she finishes telling her tale, Rose pauses for a moment. Then she adds one last thing: "He saved me in every way a person can be saved."

The life, death, and resurrection of Jesus of Nazareth answer once and for all the question, "What is God's heart toward me?" At the point of our deepest betrayal, when we had run our farthest from him and gotten so lost we could never find our way home, God came and died to rescue us. You have never been loved like this. He has come to save you in every way a person can be saved. That is God's heart toward you.

Of course, that is not the end of the Story.

It is not even the end of the act. Act Three is still under way, and we are caught up in it. A love story, set in the midst of a life-and-death battle. I will say more about this in a moment.

But now let us lift our eyes to the horizon and see what the future holds in store.

Do we have a future?

Act Four

THE KINGDOM RESTORED

See! The winter is past;
the rains are over and gone.
Flowers appear on the earth;
the season of singing has come.

—SONG OF SONGS 2:11–12

nd they lived happily ever after.

Stop for just a moment, and let it be true. *They lived happily ever after.*

These may be the most beautiful and haunting words in the entire library of mankind. Why does the end of a great story leave us with a lump in our throats and an ache in our hearts? If we haven't become entirely cynical, some of the best endings can even bring us to tears.

Because God has set eternity in our hearts. Every story we tell is our attempt to put into words and images what God has written there, on our hearts. Think of the stories that you love. Remember how they end.

Then Aslan turned to them and said, "You do not look so happy as I mean you to be."

Lucy said, "We're so afraid of being sent away, Aslan. And you have sent us back into our own world so often."

"No fear of that," said Aslan. "Have you not guessed?"

Their hearts leaped and a wild hope rose within them.

"There *was* a real railway accident," said Aslan softly. "Your father and mother and all of you are—as you used to call it in the Shadowlands— dead. The term is over: the holidays have begun. The dream is ended: this is the morning."

And as he spoke he no longer looked to them like a lion; but the things that began to happen after that were so great and beautiful I cannot write them. And for us this is the end of all the stories, and we can most truly say that they lived happily ever after. But for them it was only the beginning of the real story. All their life in this world and all their adventures in Narnia had only been the cover and the title page: now at last they were beginning Chapter One of the Great Story which no one on earth

> has read: which goes on forever: in which every
> chapter is better than the one before. (C. S.
> Lewis, *The Last Battle*)

If a story has been true to life in all its sorrow and hardness and longing, to life as we know it, and if it also offers that turn at the end in hope beyond hope, then our eyes swell with tears and we get a glimpse of Joy— Joy, as Tolkien called it, beyond the walls of this world.

What *if*?

What if this was our ending? What would it be like to have a wild hope rise within *you*?

I think of the end of the movie *Apollo 13*, based on the true story of the mission to the moon that fell to pieces, and the battle against all odds to bring those three astronauts home safely. Unknown damage has been done to the space capsule in an explosion. Their guidance system could be malfunctioning; they might miss the earth entirely. Power has been lost; their parachutes might be three blocks of ice. The heat shield that protects the men from the inferno of reentry might be cracked. Will their little ark get them home?

The world has gathered in front of televisions in homes, offices, storefronts, and schools to witness one of the greatest dramas of the twentieth century.

All radio contact is lost during the "blackout" as the command module plunges into the earth's atmosphere, hurling homeward at a speed of 35,245 feet per second. It is the final moment of their ordeal. The world is holding its collective breath, watching the sky as the news announcer states,

> No reentering ship has ever taken longer than three minutes to emerge from blackout. This is the critical moment. Will the heat shield hold? Will the command module survive the intense heat of reentry? If not . . . there'll only be . . . silence.

Men on the deck of the USS *Iwo Jima* sent to the South Pacific to rendezvous with the capsule desperately search the horizon with binoculars. In faith, navy recovery and rescue helicopters are launched. At Mission Control in Houston, all is silent. Seconds tick by like hours as the blackout continues. There is no word from the astronauts. All eyes remain fixed on the vacant sky. Flight Monitor in Houston announces the end of blackout:

> That's three minutes. Standing by for acquistion.

Mission Control attempts to contact the lost men.

Odyssey, this is Houston. Do you read me?

Silence. Only the crackling static of the radio.

Odyssey, Houston. Do you read?

Still nothing. The news anchor admits,

> The expected time of reentry has come . . .
> and gone. About all any of us can do now is
> just listen and hope.

The families of the three men are quietly holding hands. Tears begin to run down their cheeks. A few turn their eyes away, as if to avoid the inevitable. In Houston men hang their heads; they did all they could possibly do. Another full minute passes. Still nothing. The capsule is way, way beyond the point of return. The rescue has apparently failed.

Silence.

Odyssey . . . uh . . . Houston . . . do you read?

The radio begins to crackle as the television screen reveals a tiny speck emerging from the clouds. Red parachutes burst open, and we hear a reply from the command module:

> Hello, Houston . . . this is *Odyssey*. It's good to
> see you again!

Cheers. Shouts of joy. Hugs all around. Tears, tears of happiness and relief. Our boys have made it home. Flight Contact—a dear friend of the men on board—is barely able to speak.

> *Odyssey* . . . Houston. Welcome home . . . we're
> glad to see you.

And I am undone. I've seen this happy ending probably twenty times, and I weep even still. Most days I'm not even aware of how deeply I long for this as I rush through the hours of my day. But then I am stopped in my tracks by this scene, or another like it, and again I am pierced with longing. You have been, too, if you'll remember the endings of the stories you love and what it was like to hear them for the first time.

Could It Be?

This is written on the human heart, this longing for happily ever after.

You see, every story has an ending. Every story. Including yours. Have you ever faced this? Even if you do manage to find a little taste of Eden in this life, even if you are one of the fortunate souls who finds some love and happiness in the world, you cannot hang on to it. You know this. Your health cannot hold out forever. Age will conquer you. One by one your friends and loved ones will slip from your hand. Your work will remain unfinished. Your time on this stage will come to an end. Like every other person gone before you, you will breathe your last breath.

And then what? Is that the end of the Story?

If that is the end, this Story is a tragedy. Macbeth was right. Life is a tale told by an idiot, full of sound and fury, signifying nothing. Sooner or later, life will break your heart. Or rather, death will break your heart. Perhaps you have to lose someone you love to be shaken from denial. The final enemy is death. It will come. Is there no way out? Do we have a future?

Our Enemy is a thief, and of all the precious things he has stolen from our hearts, his worst act of treachery has been to steal our future from us. He has stolen all the magic and promise and wonder of the happily ever after. Very few of us live with hope. To those without faith, he has whispered, "Your story ends with an accident, and then . . . there is nothing. This is as good as it gets."

Small wonder people drink too much, eat too much, watch too much TV, basically check out. If they allow themselves to feel the depth of their actual longing for life and love and happiness, but have no hope that life will ever come . . . it's just too much to bear.

But to those who search in faith for the ending of the

Story, our Enemy has whispered an even more diabolical lie, harder to dispel because it is veiled in religious imagery: "Heaven will be a never-ending church service in the sky." All those silly images of clouds and harps. I've heard innumerable times that "we shall worship God forever." That "we shall sing one glorious hymn after another, forever and ever, amen."

It sounds like hell to me.

Seriously now—even though we *were* given Eden as our paradise, this whole wondrous world of beauty, intimacy, and adventure, in the life to come we will be sent to church forever because that's *better* somehow? There is no hope in that. That's not what's written on our hearts.

I mean, really. We have dreamed better dreams than God can dream? We have written stories that have a better ending than God has provided? It cannot be.

I have some really good news for you: that's not the so-called Good News. Not even close.

God has set eternity in our hearts. We've been trying to express it in the stories that we tell. Or rather, it has been trying to express itself, this eternity written on our hearts. And the Scripture bears witness that, in fact, the best of those stories are very close indeed to what is about to happen in *our* Story. Follow me into this. It will take your breath away.

Paradise Regained

> Then I saw a new heaven and a new earth.
> (Revelation 21:1)

Act Four also begins with light, with a dawn, revealing a Paradise.

Only, this Paradise is familiar somehow.

Picture in your mind the final scene from *Titanic*. Jack is dead, some eighty years past. Rose is now an old, old woman, her life behind her, fading like the photographs on her nightstand. We see the once great ocean liner, "the ship of dreams," crushed and rotting at the bottom of the sea. A place in each of us feels as though all stories will eventually end this way, try as we might to avoid it. All is lost.

Then something begins to happen.

Down in the darkness of the *Titanic* a light begins to break through, light as fresh and pure as the first morning of Creation. It streams in through every portal, races through every haunted place. The glorious light cleanses and restores the grandeur and beauty of the great ship before our very eyes. The rubble is swept away; the deck glistens as it did on the day it was made.

In the twinkling of an eye, the ship is *restored*. The magnificent ballroom doors swing open, and we

discover all the great hearts of the story, gathered together again. Lover and Beloved are reunited; a grand
party is under way.

This happy ending is borrowed right out of the
Scripture. An immortal life. The restoration of all
things. A wedding feast. In hope beyond hope, Paradise
is regained. This is what God has been trying to say to
us all along:

> Behold, I will create new heavens and a new
> earth. (Isaiah 65:17)

Look at the life of Jesus. Notice what he did.

When Jesus touched the blind, they could *see*; all the
beauty of the world opened before them. When he
touched the deaf, they were able to *hear*; for the first
time in their lives they heard laughter and music and
their children's voices. He touched the lame, and they
jumped to their feet and began to dance. And he called
the dead back to *life* and gave them to their families.

Do you see? Wherever humanity was broken, Jesus
restored it. He is giving us an illustration here, and
there, and there again. The coming of the kingdom of
God *restores* the world he made.

God has been whispering this secret to us through
creation itself, every year, at springtime, ever since we left

the Garden. Sure, winter has its certain set of joys. The wonder of snowfall at midnight, the rush of a sled down a hill, the magic of the holidays. But if winter ever came for good and never left, we would be desolate. Every tree leafless, every flower gone, the grasses on the hillsides dry and brittle. The world forever cold, silent, bleak.

After months and months of winter, I long for the return of summer. Sunshine, warmth, color, and the long days of adventure together. The garden blossoms in all its beauty. The meadows soft and green. Vacation. Holiday. Isn't this what we most deeply long for? To leave the winter of the world behind, what Shakespeare called "the winter of our discontent," and find ourselves suddenly in the open meadows of summer?

If we listen, we will discover something of tremendous joy and wonder. The restoration of the world played out before us each spring and summer is *precisely* what God is promising us about our lives. Every miracle Jesus ever did was pointing to this Restoration, the day he makes all things new. At the end of Act Three, he announces:

Behold, I make all things new. (Revelation 21:5 NKJV)

Behold—look at this—I am giving Paradise back to you. This is the breathtaking surprise at the end of

Titanic. And at the end of *The Lion King*—the evil one is cast down, and creation is regained, made new. So at the end of *Gladiator* we see Maximus, very much alive and healed from his many wounds, walking through the golden fields of Spain to be reunited with his wife and son. Dorothy arrives safe at home at the end of *The Wizard of Oz,* and Middle Earth is restored at the end of *The Lord of the Rings.* It is the happy end of The Chronicles of Narnia:

> It was the Unicorn who summed up what everyone was feeling. He stamped his right fore-hoof on the ground and neighed, and then cried: "I have come home at last! This is my real country! I belong here. This is the land I have been looking for all my life, though I never knew it till now. The reason why we loved the old Narnia is that it sometimes looked a little like this."

The world in all its beauty shall be ours again—forever.

TOGETHER AGAIN

And it's the word *ours* that pierces me. As I think again of the happiest endings to the best stories, I realize that what brings me to tears is the recovery of the *relationships*—the ones we have come to love are brought home again.

"O, rejoice beyond a common joy, and set it down with gold on lasting pillars." This is the cry sent up at the end of Shakespeare's play *The Tempest*. What is the reason for such uncommon rejoicing? That though treason, foul play, and a shipwreck had for so long separated families, lovers, even kingdoms, all have been reunited. In hope against hope, they have been restored to one another.

> In one voyage
> Did Claribel her husband find at Tunis,
> And Ferdinand, her brother, found a wife
> Where he himself was lost; Prospero, his dukedom
> In a poor isle; and all of us ourselves,
> When no man was his own.

It's the great company at the party in *Titanic* that brings such happy tears. It's the boys making it safely home in *Apollo 13*. It's Maximus reunited with his family. So the fellowship finds Gandalf alive—no longer Gandalf the Grey, fallen beyond recovery in the mines of Moria, but Gandalf the White, whom death can never touch again. So Frodo and Sam are rescued from the slopes of Mount Doom, and when they wake, it is to a bright new morn with the sound of birds and the laughter of their friends.

This is our future.

After he laid down his life for us, Jesus of Nazareth was laid in a tomb. He was buried just like any other dead person. His family and friends mourned. His enemies rejoiced. And most of the world went on with business as usual, clueless to the Epic around them. Then, after three days, also at dawn, his story took a sudden and dramatic turn.

> Very early on the first day of the week, just after sunrise, they were on their way to the tomb and they asked each other, "Who will roll the stone away from the entrance of the tomb?" But when they looked up, they saw that the stone, which was very large, had been rolled away. As they entered the tomb, they saw a young man dressed in a white robe sitting on the right side, and they were alarmed. "Don't be alarmed," he said. "You are looking for Jesus the Nazarene, who was crucified. He has risen! He is not here. See the place where they laid him. But go, tell his disciples . . . 'He is going ahead of you into Galilee. There you will see him, just as he told you.'" (Mark 16:2–7)

Jesus came back. He showed up again. He was restored to them. He walked into the house where they had gathered to comfort one another in their grief and asked if they had anything to eat. It was the most stunning, unbelievable, happiest ending to a story you could possibly imagine.

And it is also ours.

The resurrection of Jesus was the first of many, the forerunner of our own. He paved the way, as the saying goes.

> The fact is that Christ has been raised from the dead. He has become the first of a great harvest of those who will be raised to life again.
> (1 Corinthians 15:20 NLT)

> God knew what he was doing from the very beginning. He decided from the outset to shape the lives of those who love him along the same lines as the life of his Son. The Son stands first in the line of humanity he restored.
> (Romans 8:29 *The Message*)

So we, too, shall live and never die. Creation will be restored, and *we* will be restored. And we shall share it together. "Today," Jesus said to the thief on the cross, "you will be with me in paradise" (Luke 23:43).

Imagine that. Imagine being reunited with the ones you love, and with all the great and noble hearts of this Story, in paradise.

We will walk with God in the Garden in the cool of the day. We will see our Jesus face-to-face. We will hear him laugh. All that has ever stood between us will be swept away, and our hearts will be released to real loving. It begins with a great party, just as in *Titanic*, what the Scriptures call the "wedding feast of the Lamb" (Revelation 19:9 NLT). You'll raise a glass with Adam and Eve, with Paul and St. Patrick, with your grandmother and your grandson.

Imagine the stories that you'll hear. And all the questions that shall finally have answers. And the answers won't be one-word answers, but story after story, a feast of wonder and laughter and glad tears.

WILL EVERYONE I LOVE BE THERE?

The kingdom of heaven is like a king who prepared a wedding banquet for his son. He sent his servants to those who had been invited to the banquet to tell them to come, but they refused to come. Then he sent some more servants and said, "Tell those who have been

> invited that I have prepared my dinner . . .
> Come to the wedding banquet." But they paid
> no attention and went off—one to his field,
> another to his business. (Matthew 22:2–5)

Now for a sobering truth, more sobering than any other we have considered.

To be honest, we must understand that not everyone lives happily ever after, not in any tale. This promise of the happy ending—or the new beginning—is only for the friends of God. Many people do not want the life that God offers them. If they would reject the very Heart of all things, well, then, where shall they spend their eternity?

Many awful things have been done with the doctrine of hell. "You'll go to hell for that" has been used to condemn all sorts of things that God does not condemn. You know . . . "Don't smoke, don't chew, don't go with girls who do." And although the Bible condemns *drunkenness*, it also says that wine gladdens the heart of man (Psalm 104:15). And may I add that during the last meal he shared with his friends before his death, Jesus said, "Mark my words—I will not drink wine again until the day I drink it new with you in my Father's Kingdom" (Matthew 26:29 NLT). There'll be wine at the Banquet.

Furthermore, those who have swung the idea of hell around like a club give you the impression that they'll be glad to see you sent there. But not our God, who "is patient with you, not wanting anyone to perish, but everyone to come to repentance" (2 Peter 3:9). The Lover of our souls, the One who has pursued us down through space and time, who gave his own life to rescue us from the Kingdom of Darkness, has made it clear: He does not want to lose us. He longs for us to be with him forever.

Nonetheless, simply because certain people have abused the concept of hell doesn't mean it doesn't exist.

First, you must understand that hell was created not for mankind, but for Satan and his angels (Matthew 25:41). I'm sure you'll remember with relish the stories where the evil one is destroyed in the end. Commodus being slain with his own knife in the arena. Darth Maul falling to the saber of Obi-Wan Kenobi. A great chasm opening in the earth to swallow Sauron and his army of Orcs so that Middle Earth might be free at last.

Hell is not God's intention for mankind.

But remember—he gave us free will.

He gave us a choice.

We seem to forget—perhaps more truthfully, we refuse to remember—that we are the ones who betrayed him, not vice versa. We are the ones who listened to the lies of the Evil One in the Garden; we chose to mistrust the heart of God. In breaking the one command he gave us, we set in motion a life of breaking his commands. (You have loved God with all your heart, soul, mind, and strength? You have loved your neighbor as yourself?)

The final act of self-centeredness is seen in those who refuse to come to the wedding banquet of God (Matthew 22:2–3). They do not want God. They reject his offer of forgiveness and reconciliation through Jesus. What is he to do? The universe has only two options. If they insist, God will grant to them what they have wanted—to be left to themselves.

> The man wakes from the final struggle of death, in absolute loneliness—such a loneliness as in the most miserable moment of deserted childhood he never knew. Not a hint, not a shadow of anything outside his consciousness reaches him. All is dark, dark and dumb; no motion—not the breath of a wind! Never a dream of change! Not a scent from far-off field! No sign of God anywhere. God has so far withdrawn from the man . . . he is in God's prison, his own separated self.
>
> (George MacDonald, *The Last Farthing*)

To be rescued from an eternity apart from God—
this is why the rescued ones fall before him at the
Great Feast in songs of gratitude and worship. Yes, we
will worship God. It won't be like a church service,
but we will worship him. We will adore him.

But that day has not yet come.

Until then, the invitation of life stands.

> I have set before you life and death . . . Now
> choose life. (Deuteronomy 30:19)

LIFE AT LAST

And life *is* the offer, friends. Let us not forget that.

> For God so loved the world that he gave his one
> and only Son, that whoever believes in him shall
> not perish but have eternal life. (John 3:16)

> Come to me to have life. (John 5:40)

> The thief comes only to steal and kill and
> destroy; I have come that they may have life,
> and have it to the full. (John 10:10)

> This is the way to have eternal life—to know

> you, the only true God, and Jesus Christ, the
> one you sent to earth. (John 17:3 NLT)

> Whoever is thirsty, let him come; and whoever
> wishes, let him take the free gift of the water
> of life. (Revelation 22:17)

There is no simpler or more beautiful way to say it
than this: Act Four is the restoration of life as it was
always meant to be.

It is the return of the beauty, the intimacy, and
the adventure we were created to enjoy and have
longed for every day of our lives. And yet, *better*, for
it is immortal. We can never lose it again. It cannot
be taken away. Sunrise and sunset tell the tale every
day, remembering Eden's glory, foretelling Eden's
return.

And what adventures shall unfold when we are
given the kingdom that was always meant to be ours.
Listen to this:

> Then the King will say to those on his right,
> "Come, you who are blessed by my Father;
> take your inheritance, *the kingdom prepared for*
> *you since the creation of the world*." (Matthew
> 25:34, emphasis added)

> Who then is the faithful and wise servant,
> whom the master has put in charge of the ser-
> vants in his household to give them their food
> at the proper time? It will be good for that ser-
> vant whose master finds him doing so when he
> returns. I tell you the truth, *he will put him in*
> *charge of all his possessions.* (Matthew 24:45–47,
> emphasis added)

Adam and Eve, and all their sons and daughters
after them, were created to reign over the earth—to
explore and discover and create and do all those things
you see people do when they are at their very best.

That is our destiny.

If all we have are clouds and harps, our options are
pretty limited. But to have the whole cosmos before
us—wow! Christ is not joking when he says that we
shall inherit the kingdom prepared for us and we shall
reign with him forever. We will take the position for
which we have been uniquely made and will rule *as he*
does—meaning, with creativity and power.

> The created world itself can hardly wait for
> what's coming next. Everything in creation is
> being more or less held back. God reins it in
> until both creation and all the creatures are ready

and can be released at the same moment into
the glorious times ahead. (Romans 8: 19–20
The Message)

All creation anticipates the day when it will
join God's children in glorious freedom from
death and decay. (Romans 8:21 NLT)

What would you like to do first? Paddle a canoe
down the Amazon? Learn to play an instrument?
Discover a new universe? You'll have plenty of time
for that and more.

And in the perfect time, O perfect God,
When we are in our home, our natal home,
When joy shall carry every sacred load,
And from its life and peace no heart shall roam,
What if thou make us able to make like thee—
To light with moons, to clothe with greenery,
To hang gold sunsets o'er a rose and purple sea!
(George MacDonald, *Diary of an Old Soul*)

WILL WE MAKE IT?

Several years into our marriage, Stasi and I reached
one of the lowest moments of our lives.

As we were sitting at the breakfast table one morning, the subject of divorce was raised in a rather casual way, as if it were a question about the raspberry jam. We had drifted apart—I knew that—but until that moment I didn't realize just how far. Over the next few days I made an emergency plan. We would go to the mountains for a holiday in hopes of recovering some of the ground we had lost. We had honeymooned in Yosemite, and I thought that might be the place to look again for our lost romance.

We set out the day after Christmas on a warm and sunny morning. But as the hours wore on, a snowstorm was building in the mountains ahead. Evening fell, and with it came the snow, softly at first, then heavier and harder. Our car began to slip and spin on the icy road. It was dark when we reached the entrance to the park. Up ahead, I could see the cars before us turning around and heading back down the mountain. *Oh, Lord*, I prayed, *please—not now, not when so much is hanging on this*. The ranger told us that the roads had become treacherous, and a blizzard was raging higher in the mountains. Several cars had already slid off the highway. He recommended we turn back but left the choice to us.

"We're going on," I said.

As the hours dragged on, snow covered the road and

woods all around. We were totally alone in a dark forest. *Will we make it?* I wondered to myself. *Can it possibly be good even if we do?* My knuckles were white from clutching the steering wheel. The tension in the car was thick, a very real reminder of the reason we had come.

Just when I was about to abandon hope, twinkling lights appeared through the trees ahead. As we rounded the bend, the hotel came into view—a gorgeous white Victorian inn with garlands hanging from the balcony and a massive Christmas tree in the window. The snowfall had let up, and the flakes were falling softly, gently. We could see a fire roaring in the large stone fireplace, casting a romantic glow over the couples who lingered over dinner.

As I pulled our car into safety, a deer ambled from the woods and across the white meadow before us.

We had made it.

The beauty of it all seemed to speak the promise of a life restored. As we walked into our room, we discovered a bottle of champagne on ice—a gift some friends had sent ahead. That weekend we turned a corner in our marriage; we did not divorce. That was twenty years ago. It has been quite a journey toward restoration, but restoration has come.

For now, our life is a journey of high stakes and frequent danger. But we are nearing the end of Act

Three; certainly we are nearing the end of our scene in it. The long years in exile are winding down, and we are approaching home. There is no longer any question about whether we will make it and whether it will be good when we get there. "I am going there to prepare a place for you," Jesus promised. "And if I go and prepare a place for you, I will come back and take you to be with me" (John 14:2–3).

One day soon we will round a bend in the road, and our dreams will come true. We really will live happily ever after. The long years in exile will be swept away in the joyful tears of our arrival home. Every day when we rise, we can tell ourselves, *My journey today will bring me closer to home; it may be just around the bend.* All we long for, we shall have; all we long to be, we will be. All that has hurt us so deeply will be swept away.

And then real life begins.

> We can most truly say that they lived happily ever after. But for them it was only the beginning of the real story . . . now at last they were beginning Chapter One of the Great Story which no one on earth has read: which goes on forever: in which every chapter is better than the one before. (*The Last Battle*)

THE ROAD BEFORE US

The Road goes ever on and on
Down from the door where it began.
Now far ahead the Road has gone,
And I must follow, if I can,
Pursuing it with eager feet,
Until it joins some larger way.

— J. R. R. TOLKIEN

nd now?

Now we are living somewhere toward the end of Act Three. We have a future, but this tale is not over yet—not by a long shot. We now live between the battle for Helm's Deep and the Battle of the Pelennor Fields. Between the beaches of Normandy and the end of the war. Between the fall of the Republic and the fall of the Empire. Between Paradise lost and Paradise regained.

We live in a far more dramatic, far more dangerous Story than we ever imagined. The reason we love The Chronicles of Narnia or *Star Wars* or *The Matrix* or

The Lord of the Rings is because they are telling us something about our lives that we never, ever get on the evening news. Or from most pulpits. They are reminding us of the Epic we are created for.

This is the sort of tale you've fallen into. How would you live differently if you believed it to be true?

The final test of any belief or faith that claims to provide an answer to our lives is this: Does the one explain the other? Does the story bring into perspective the pages you were already holding, the days of your life? Does it take everything into account? Does it explain the longing in your heart for a life you haven't yet found? Does it explain the evil cast around us? Most of all, does it give you back your heart, lead you to the Source of life?

Something has been calling to you all the days of your life. You've heard it on the wind and in the music you love, in laughter and in tears, and most especially in the stories that have ever captured your heart. There *is* a secret written on your heart. A valiant Hero-Lover and his Beloved. An Evil One and a great battle to fight. A Journey and a Quest, more dangerous and more thrilling than you could imagine. A little Fellowship to see you through.

This is the gospel of Christianity.

Now—what is *your* part? What is your role in the Story?

In truth, the only one who can tell you that is the Author. To find our lives, we must turn to Jesus. We must yield our all to him and ask him to restore us as his own. We ask his forgiveness for our betrayal of him. We ask him to make us all he intended us to be—to tell us who we are and what we are now to do. We ask him to remove the veil from our eyes and from our hearts. It might be good to pause and do that right now.

> A veil covers their hearts. But whenever anyone turns to the Lord, the veil is taken away. (2 Corinthians 3:15–16)

> We do this by keeping our eyes on Jesus, on whom our faith depends from start to finish. He was willing to die a shameful death on the cross because of the joy he knew would be his afterward. Now he is seated in the place of highest honor beside God's throne in heaven. (Hebrews 12:2 NLT)

REMEMBER

The Story God is telling—like every great story that echoes it—reminds us of three eternal truths it would be good to keep in mind as we take the next step out the door.

First, *things are not what they seem.*

Where would we be if Eve had recognized the serpent for who he really was? And that carpenter from Nazareth—he's not what he appears to be, either. There is far more going on around us than meets the eye. We live in a world with two halves, one part that we can see and another part that we cannot. We must live as though the unseen world (the rest of reality) is more weighty and more real and more dangerous than the part of reality we can see.

Second, *we are at war.*

This is a love Story, set in the midst of a life-and-death battle. Just look around you. Look at all the casualties strewn across the field. The lost souls, the broken hearts, the captives. We must take this battle seriously. This is no child's game. This is war—a battle for the human heart.

Third, *you have a crucial role to play.*

That is the third eternal truth spoken by every great story, and it happens to be the one we most desperately need if we are ever to understand our days. Frodo underestimated who he was. As did Neo. As did Wallace. As did Peter, James, and John. It is a dangerous thing to underestimate your role in the Story. You will lose heart, and you will miss your cues.

This is our most desperate hour. You are needed.

We are now far into this Epic that every great story points to. We have reached the moment where we, too, must find our courage and rise up to recover our hearts and fight for the hearts of others. The hour is late, and much time has been wasted. Aslan is on the move; we must rally to him at the stone table. We must find Geppetto lost at sea. We must ride hard, ride to Minas Tirith and join the last great battle for Middle Earth.

Jesus calls to you to be his intimate ally once more. There are great things to be done and great sacrifices to be made. You won't lose heart if you know what's really going on here, where this Story is headed and what your Lover has promised to you.

> It is a world of magic and mystery, of deep darkness and flickering starlight. It is a world where terrible things happen and wonderful things too. It is a world where goodness is pitted against evil, love against hate, order against chaos, in a great struggle where often it is hard to be sure who belongs to which side because appearances are endlessly deceptive. Yet for all its confusion and wildness, it is a world where the battle goes ultimately to the good, who live happily ever after, and where in the long run

everybody, good and evil alike, becomes known by his true name . . . That is the fairy tale of the Gospel with, of course, one crucial difference from all other fairy tales, which is that the claim made for it is that it is true, that it not only happened once upon a time but has kept on happening ever since and is happening still. (*Telling the Truth*)

This is the gospel.
This is the Story we are living in.
May you play your part well.